Echoes of Empathy

Farhan Chaudhary

BookLeaf
Publishing
India | USA | UK

Presentation by *BookLeaf Publishing*

Web: www.bookleafpub.com

E-mail: info@bookleafpub.com

ISBN: 9789358737011

First edition 2023

*I dedicate this book to all those who suffer from
negative self-talk and need inner child healing;
I hope you find the power of being kind to self,
setting boundaries and living life with gratitude
through these words.*

ACKNOWLEDGEMENT

To the one who introduced me to reading, Fauzia Chaudhary, my sister, your support and encouragement to read and write and your belief in the power of words have helped me give voice to echoes of empathy. Your constant reminder to be kind to others even in pain led me to self-discovery.

To my brother Faizan Chaudhary, who has supported my endeavours with patience and helped me build resilience. Also, thanks for buying all the books that I could steal.

To my family, Mom, Dad, my sister-in-law Sayyada Chaudhary, my niece and my nephew, whose presence in my life has made it easier to live with gratitude.

To my therapist, who helped me embark on this healing journey.

Lastly, to Amrita, my dearest friend and ex-wife, you have believed in me and took a chance with me to help me grow into this person who can reflect, write and talk about feelings, be vulnerable and inspire me to lead an authentic life.

PREFACE

In the quiet corners of my soul and my healing journey, I have embarked upon this journey to find my authentic self through therapy and self-help books. While I was reading these books and doing the work, I was inspired to write poetry about topics that have helped me with my healing in the hopes that it would inspire me and others to continue doing the work.

Embracing oneself with love, compassion, and kindness is the central theme of this book. I have taken cues from my personal life and my interactions with friends and family to find solace in the journey of growth.

As you journey through these poems, I hope that you will find echoes of empathy resonating with your heart. May it inspire you to reach out to your inner child and others with compassion, to listen intently and to discover the transformative power of kindness.

Thank you for joining me on this journey.

With warmest regards,
Farhan Chaudhary

Art of Authenticity

Whenever they felt small and less, a tiny
whisper gnawed in their head,
"Fake it till you make it," it said
They wear the mask, become a part of the
charade,
Feigning confidence, afraid to have their true
self displayed

In the early days, the little person conceals,
Afraid that people would find what an unhappy
family reveals,
With a troubled young heart, shadows collide,
Both bullied and a bully, their pain they hide,
They fake it behind angst, indifference and
laughter
They make it smiling but live through a blur

As adulthood unfolds, inner voids expand,
External love insufficient to fill spaces so grand.
Only through shattered hearts can reconstruction
commence,
Yet, fleeting are these borrowed instances of
recompense.

With the weight of grief, the shield of pretense
becomes harder to carry,
Seeking help and being vulnerable, they are no
more wary,
No more hiding, no more fear, embracing quirks,
forgiving flaws,
The beauty of being, in authenticity, the spirit
thaws

They reach here through grief, some through
love, a few through self-hate and doubt,
Whatever one's journey is, the art of authenticity
is on your route,
There is a lifetime of self-love to embrace,
For in being one's true self, we all shall find
Grace.

Building Boundaries

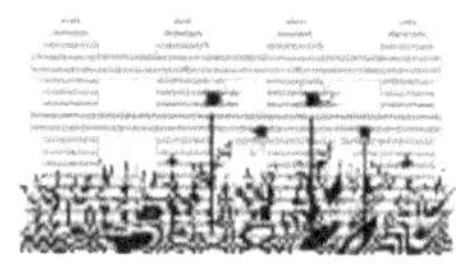

From the art of authenticity,
We begin to lay the foundation of boundaries,
With the bricks of self-compassion
And cement of love and passion,
From our windows of vulnerability, we welcome
the soothing breeze,
We fill up the space in our rooms with
individuality and honesty.

A sacred space for self, with respect for others,
We construct those walls to protect our hearts,
Firm boundaries that don't obstruct our growth,
Our sanctuary is a reminder of our self-worth,
It helps us face, cope and embrace life,
It gives us hope, Grace, and it does suffice.

Remember to keep a garden of kindness,
Stand tall and welcoming in your garden,
A sense of wonder fills you about the blue skies,

When there are clouds that bring those blues,
Retrieve within and be your own Guardian,
The boundaries that you built will bring you
happiness.

Creating Compassion

Compassion for self and others binds the heart
and head together,
Sometimes living inside your head can be a
bother,
Shared humanity helps you heal and grow,
Creating compassion to let your heart glow.

When we open our souls, we witness love
beyond compare,
A genuine desire to help others, our actions full
of care,
In this journey of life, we are all entwined,
Creating compassion, the world redefined.

In every gesture, big and small,
Compassion leaps and reaches over the walls,
With open arms, we embrace ourselves and
others,

Creating compassion, a love that endlessly
hovers.

When we go beyond sympathy's veil,
We extend our hands to the weary and frail,
We reach out to help others but heal our hearts
Creating compassion and mending our broken
parts

Dynamism of Diversity

Every culture has a story to tell,
If you open the doors and answer the bell,
Broadening horizons, we venture far and wide,
Exploring new places with our eyes open wide

Even when you are bound by circumstance,
Give space to happenstance,
Listen to views that differ from your own,
Your life plants encompass all when diverse
seeds are sown

With open minds we seek to learn,
With a medley of thoughts we discern,
Our compassion, empathy and humility grow,
We adapt, change and recognise our flow

Living a wholesome life with a hunger to know,

People, places, purpose accepting the goodness
that life throws,
Taking me closer to authenticity as I know
myself and others,
The dynamism of diversity creates a life of
wonder.

Echoes of Empathy

Walking in someone else's shoes, we try to see,
Their struggles, their joys, what it means to be free,
An extended hand, an open heart and a free soul,
A gift we can offer, a mutual goal

When we are caught up in a circle of despair,
Someone entering in with Empathy and care,
Guides us towards what's good and right,
In Empathy's inner ring, compassion takes flight

We seek eternal life and immortal glow,
But we find it within when Empathy flows,
Hidden secrets lose power in any room,
In Empathy's grace, visible revelations bloom.

Through tears that fall like rain, we feel another's ache,
In silence and words, their solace we partake,
With kindness as our guide, we mend what's torn apart,
Empathy's gentle touch is a balm for every heart.

Empathy's gentle song,
It plays through the soul, making us strong,
Building hearts together, showing that we care,
Echoes of Empathy, a melody rare.

Fortitude of Friendship

When I ran away from something, I ran towards
a friend,
When I ran towards something, I needed a friend
till the end,
My muffled screams and triumphant laughs,
Shared with someone who walks life's winding
paths.

Some stayed on this journey for long,
Few left behind where they belong,
In each chapter written, a story that teaches,
Leaving footprints of memories on mountains
and beaches

Through ups and downs, they stood by my side,
In their unwavering presence, I found my guide.
Their laughter a balm, their silence a sanctuary,
A bond of trust and love, never temporary.

In shared secrets and dreams, we found our
retreat,
A shelter from life's chaos, a connection so
sweet.
Hand in hand, we faced trials and sunlit skies,
Growing stronger together, with each sunrise.

Through trials and triumphs, side by side we
stand,
A fortitude of friendship, unbreakable and
grand.
In laughter and in tears, our bond remains
strong,
A connection that endures, where we truly
belong.

Grace of Gratitude

Every night when I sit with my journal at the end
of the day,
I remember three things I was grateful for today,
At times I sit for a long time and struggle with
shame,
But most days, it's the food I ate, a kind gesture, a
challenge I overcame.

In Gratitude, I find grace every day,
the simplest of joys light up my way,
A whispered thanks in the moment I felt grateful,
In those moments life feels full.

For even in hardships, lessons we find,
A chance to grow, a shift in our mind.
With grateful eyes, we see life's rich hue,
The grace of gratitude, forever true.

When I look back at my journal entries,
I laugh, cry, moments of reverie,

Gratitude is etched in each page,
Preparing me for any of life's stages.

Grace of gratitude helps me soar,
Through life's highs and challenges, I explore.
With thankful heart and open eyes,
I find joy in moments, big and wise

Harmony of Healing

Harmony of healing after a tumultuous tide,
A journey of rediscovery, hearts open wide.
Scars slowly fade, as time gently weaves,
New beginnings arise, like autumn's golden leaves.

Echoes of laughter replace sorrow's refrain,
In the tapestry of healing, we find strength to
regain.
Through tear-stained nights and hopeful dawns,
We learn to mend what once was torn.

Forgiveness blooms like flowers in spring,
A balm for the wounds that once did sting.
In the spaces between, we breathe anew,
Reclaiming our essence, finding skies so blue.

The road to healing winds, takes its own pace,
But in its twists and turns, we find grace.
With each step forward, we break free,
From the chains of pain, embracing destiny.

Through this journey of healing, we emerge anew,
With scars as badges of strength, tried and true.
Harmony finds us as wounds softly mend,
After a scarring chapter, we begin again

Insights for Inner Child

In healing's embrace, the inner child speaks,
Whispering secrets, long hidden, but not weak.
Lessons of innocence, untouched by time,
In the depths of the past, they gently chime.

Through laughter and tears, she shows the way,
Revealing wounds healed or still in disarray.
Lessons of resilience, learned in days of old,
A treasure trove of wisdom, a story to be told.

In shadows and light, the inner child thrives,
Unveiling the past, where vulnerability survives.
Lessons of acceptance, to nurture and to care,
Guiding us through healing, teaching us to
repair.

Through a kind lens, the inner child's view,
Lessons in compassion, for ourselves anew.
In her laughter and whispers, we find the way,
Guiding us towards wholeness, come what may.

Journey of Joy

A journey of joy, a path we walk,
Through fields of laughs, where worries are lost.
Each step is music, every moment a tune,
In life's big song, where we all are in soon.

Through bright fields and skies above,
We find happiness in all we love.
Dancing through times, both little and big,
On a happy trip, where all moments are big.

With laughs together and hugs so tight,
Joy's magic appears, shining light.
Through friendships made and hearts so close,
On a happy trip, we find what matters most.

Let's keep going, with heads held up high,
Under the joyous sky, aiming for the sky.
A road full of surprises, with moments that surprise,
Our big adventure, the journey of life.

Knowledge of Kindness

Learn about kindness, like a light that glows,
Plant seeds of caring, watch how it grows.
It's a way to be nice, showing others you care,
Found everywhere in life, here and there.

With words and actions, easy and clear,
Kindness builds friendships, drawing others near.
It's smart to be kind, with no limit in sight,
Speaking heart to heart, making things right.

A smile, a helping hand, in little things we do,
Kindness is a word everyone can understand too.
As we learn to be good, it's a gift we can give,
Teaching how to be kind is a great way to live.

Kindness lessons are big and important to share,
Like ripples in water, spreading everywhere.
When things are tough, kindness is a shining light,
Making everything feel okay and bright.

So, let's spread kindness, let it grow tall and wide,
With every act of caring, let your spirit ride.
When you know its power, you will see,
Kindness changes the world, gently and
beautifully.

Lovingness of Listening

When we truly listen, it's a way to bond,
Like a music tune or a magic wand.
With open ears and no rush in the air,
Friendships grow strong and fair.

Taking time to hear stories unfold,
In the act of listening, love takes hold.
It's a precious thing, kind and sweet,
In the quiet moment, love takes a seat.

Each story told adds a line to life's page,
With love for listening, it's like setting a stage.
No harsh words, just understanding and care,
A safe place for all, with moments to spare.

With quiet whispers and feelings that flow,
Through love of listening, friendships grow.
It's a bridge between hearts, connecting the line,
Where care blossoms and moments are fine.

So, let's keep this art close and always in mind,
With love for listening, treasures we find.
It's a dance of connection, with love in the
design,
Through listening closely, we let our kindness
shine.

Multitudes of Mindfulness

Lots of mindfulness, like a quiet sea,
A place where thoughts are calm and free.
Living in the now, learning to just "be",
With each breath we take, we feel more free.

Our senses wake up, we see things bright,
Colors pop, and every sound feels right.
Lots of mindfulness, like a trip inside,
Finding out where real peace does hide.

Each step on Earth feels special and sound,
Being in the moment, with all the sights and sounds.
A quiet spot in the middle of busy and fast,
Where mindfulness grows, and stress is in the past.

In this cool space, worries take a break,
We find quiet in the moment, make no mistake.
Through lots of mindfulness, we get the turn,
To enjoy every moment, it's what we learn.

So let's learn about this big, kind space,
Where mindfulness happens, it's a great place.
A way to be really present, a treasure we find,
With every breath, it's peace of mind.

Nourishment of Now

Living in the "now" is food for the heart,
In each moment, that's where we start.
Tasting life's good stuff, feeling all around,
With every breath, we find things that astound.

Forget the past and what's coming, let them go,
Just enjoy this moment, let your feelings show.
Living in the "now" is a gift, so fine,
In its warm hug, we straighten and align.

No stress about yesterday, or what's coming
next,
Living in the "now" is simple, not complex.
A party of being present, feeling alive,
In this special "now" moment, we all high-five.

Opulence of Open-Mindedness

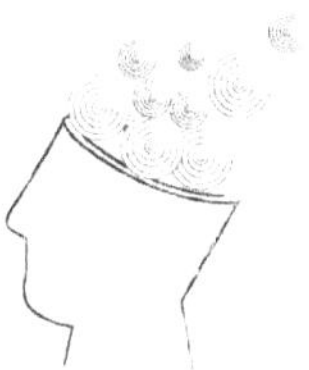

Opulence of open-mindedness, a treasure untold,
A realm where perspectives intermingle and unfold.
Riches of understanding, free from judgment's chain,
In this opulent state, hearts and minds gain.

An abundance of empathy, blossoming wide,
In the garden of open thoughts, prejudice can't hide.
Open to learning, to ideas yet unseen,
Opulence of open-mindedness, a realm serene.

In its wealth, bridges are built, connections rise,
Breaking down barriers, unveiling new skies.
A bounty of growth, where wisdom resides,
Opulence of open-mindedness, a beacon that guides.

So let's embrace this opulence, open and free,
Unlocking doors of possibility for you and me.
In open-mindedness, we truly explore,
A wealth of perspectives, forever to adore.

Power of Play

Like children chasing the summer sun,
In the power of play, we're all young.
A respite from worries, a care's release,
It infuses life with a sense of peace.

Through games and laughter, hearts connect,
In the power of play, life's colors reflect.
It's in these moments, so simple and free,
That we truly become who we're meant to be.

A break from routines, a way to explore,
In the power of play, we find so much more.
An elixir for stress, a remedy sweet,
A dance with life that makes us complete.

So let's embrace this power, with hearts open
wide,
In the playground of life, let our spirits guide.
For in the joy of play, we find our way,
To a vibrant existence, every single

Quest for Quietude

In a world of notifications, buzzing non-stop,
Amidst social media clamor, many wish it'd just drop.
Beyond the tweets, past the endless scroll,
The quest for quietude becomes the soul's goal.
Whispers of real life, drowned in virtual song,
Seeking true connection, where do we belong?
Finding solace away from the digital rush,
Seeking a moment of stillness, a genuine hush.
Amidst the online chatter, the heart yearns to retreat,
Where authenticity and inner peace can discreetly meet.
On this quest for quiet, amidst the online sound,
It's away from the screens that true calm is found.

Radiance of Reflection

In reflection's glow, our souls become clear,
With quiet pondering, unveiled truths appear.
Venturing inward, watching thoughts soar,
Insights bubble up, revealing more.

With a pause, vision sharpens, gaining clarity,
Unpacking layers, acknowledging reality.
Delving into introspection, unraveling the
mysterious,
Contemplating life's essence, feeling curious.

Memory's canvas displays various hues,
Dancing gently as we peruse.
Absorbing lessons, celebrating growth's gain,
Sustained spirits, thriving amid life's terrain.

Embarking on self-discovery, steering diligently,
Integrating aspects discovered, acting
intentionally.
Recognizing our uniqueness, appreciating the
grand design,
Crafted mosaic of experiences, exquisitely
intertwine.

Allow the radiant reflection to illuminate the
way,
Side by side, traversing, learning every day.
Connecting deeply, understanding's beacon ever
bright,
In reflection's tender arms, we encounter the
right.

Symphony of service

Hey, gather 'round, let's get this straight,
A "Symphony of Service", with no room for
hate.
Together we join, standing side by side,
Offering help, with arms open wide.

Not just about giving; it's how we live,
Creating change we see, with lots to give.
From hearts to streets, with a kindness melody,
In this "Symphony of Service", living happily.

Big or small, every helping deed lands,
Building connections, turning frowns to bands.
Spreading good vibes, passing it all around,
In the symphony, where love and care are found.

Whatever the vibe, whatever the groove,
Singing songs of care, making all improve.
Joining hearts together with notes oh-so-sweet,
In the "Symphony of Service", where love and
rhythm meet.

Hand in hand, from places near and far,
Creating a better world, under the same star.
It's not just music; it's the legacy we leave,
In the symphony, where we all believe.
Keep the music playing, let kindness freely
stream,
Singing unity, with a helping theme.
Playing the symphony of service, from morning
to night,
With every act of love, making the world bright.

Tenderness of Therapy

In the tenderness of therapy, a sacred space,
Hearts find solace, minds embrace.
Guided by gentle words, unspoken fears unfold,
In this haven of healing, stories are told.

A connection that nurtures, a bond that mends,
In the tenderness of therapy, wounds find
amends.
With empathy's touch, wounds start to mend,
As the journey within takes a loving bend.

Through tears and triumphs, we navigate,
In the tenderness of therapy, we cultivate.
A sanctuary for growth, a haven for release,
In the hands of compassion, we find our peace.

So let's honor this tenderness, pure and true,
In the realm of therapy, where healing ensues.
A journey of rediscovery, a path to reclaim,
In the tenderness of therapy, we'll never be the
same.

Unboxing Understanding

In a world of layers, dense and deep,
"Understanding" is a secret we seek to keep.
Unboxing it, a challenge profound,
Yet within its depths, truths are found.
With every layer we dare to peel,
Emotions emerge, raw and real.
Questions arise, answers unfold,
Stories of struggles, tales untold.
To unbox is to embark on a quest,
Seeking clarity, laying doubts to rest.
Each revelation, a step towards the light,
Guiding us through the darkest night.
Wisps of wisdom while in a dance,
Unlocking chains, enabling self-romance,
Embrace the journey, take understanding's hand,
For in its embrace, we truly understand

Virtues of Vulnerability

Listen up, here's something true,
Vulnerability's a strength that can empower you.
It's being open and honest, building trust that
lasts,
Where realness shines and healing happens fast.

Walls we've built, they start to fall away,
When we embrace vulnerability each day.
It takes a brave heart to show feelings and more,
In this special space, we all can explore.

Showing we're not perfect, facing the unknown,
That's when vulnerability's power is shown.
It's a bridge between hearts, a connection deep,
Where understanding and love are ours to keep.

By sharing our struggles, we find we're set free,
Vulnerability's a path where our spirits agree.
It's all about growing, learning to be true,
When we're really ourselves, doors open anew.

Wonders of Wholesomeness

In the world of wholesomeness, so good and kind,
We find pure moments that gently bind.
Simple smiles, laughter that's bright,
Walking through goodness, feeling just right.

With kindness leading, hearts open up wide,
Wholesomeness is where love likes to hide.
Laughter shared, reaching out a hand,
In a wholesome world, together we stand.

It's a quiet place away from a busy day,
Where wholesomeness helps keep worry away.
With harmony playing, like a song so sweet,
In this good place, joy is on repeat.

Let's celebrate wholesomeness, with its gentle grace,
Here, we all have a special place.
With threads of goodness, light shining bright,
In a wholesome world, everything's alright.

X-Raying Existence

In a world of mirrored mysteries profound,
X-raying existence, we seek what's unbound.
Peering past surfaces, layers and sheen,
Diving deep where the unseen is seen.
X-rays of thought pierce the opaque night,
Revealing hidden truths, bringing them to light.
Each secret unveiled, each story retold,
Glimpses of tales both young and old.
Yet, as we scan life's intricate dance,
Some enigmas elude even the keenest glance.
For in the vast expanse of all we survey,
Mysteries remain, tucked safely away.
In this journey, both vast and intense,
We celebrate the wonder of x-raying existence.

Yielding to Yearning

In the heart of a youth, dreams begin to play,
Yearning for adventures, come what may.
Each day feels like a story, fresh and new,
Yielding moments, some fleeting, some true.
Desires dance, like fireflies in the night,
Young hopes glowing, oh so bright!
Every laugh, every tear, a song unsung,
Yearnings of a heart, so very young.
To explore, to dream, to take a turn,
Yearning's fire will always burn.
For in the journey of young dreams,
Yielding to yearning is where magic is seen.

Zestful Zeal

In the zigzag pathways of life's maze,
Zeal emerges, setting the heart ablaze.
With zest, every moment becomes a dance,
Zipping through challenges, taking a chance.
Zodiacs may shift, and stars may align,
Yet zeal remains, forever the spine.
For when zest and passion in hearts freeze,
Zeal, like a phoenix, flies in the breeze.
Even when the zenith seems far and high,
Zest carries us, letting spirits fly.
In life's zestful dance, always be keen,
For zeal is the magic, rarely seen.

Any work of Mental Health is not useful till it's not put into practice, below are poems A-Z in Practice with personal examples in my life and some people that I have seen put this to practice/ situations I wish they could be used.

Art of Authenticity- A Glimpse of Reality

She always hid behind her radiant smile,
While her heart battled storms mile by mile.
Outside, she'd laugh, yet at home she'd weep,
Struggling with secrets she felt she must keep.
But with time, she chose to shed her disguise,
Are you feeling "Okay" "No" she said,
Speaking her truth, letting Authenticity rise

Building Boundaries –
Finally Feeling Free

Once she was always the yes dove,
Putting others' needs and whims above.
But one day, at work, she felt her spirit wane,
Realized her worth wasn't tied to others' gain.
She set boundaries, strong and clear,
Finding strength, letting go of fear.
Now in her garden of self-worth she stands,
Guarded boundaries drawn in life's shifting
sands.

Creating Compassion- Stories shared in silence

At the college library, she often read,
Lost in books, letting her imagination spread.
One day, she noticed him, his eyes welled with tears,
Walked up to him, shared her favourite story, easing his fears.
Through books and kind words, their bond did start,
Creating compassion, a friendship with an open heart

Dynamism of Diversity – First Day of University

On her first day of university,
She feared being made fun of or shown pity.
She hailed from a land, her accent defined,
But her thoughts and actions, truly refined.
She saw many like herself, aiming to belong,
From varied lands, echoing a unique song.
As moments passed, they all began to see,
In their diversity, they found unity.

Echoes of Empathy - A Healing Remedy

In the midst of the COVID tide,
She felt so confined, isolated in her room,
anxieties intertwined.
Across the world, he was in quarantine too,
Zoom catch-ups, shared playlists and books,
gestures kind and true.
They'd talk of hope, and brighter days ahead,
His words of comfort, a salve for the dread.
Though miles apart, their spirits felt so near,
In the echoes of empathy, they found solace
from fear.

Fortitude of Friendship - Tea Time Tales

Every Sunday at the corner cafe,
They met, come what may.
School buddies from the age of ten,
Now in their sixties, they reminisced again.
They laughed over childhood pranks and teen
year dreams,
Shared stories of grandchildren and life's
everchanging streams.
Their bond, time-tested, through joys and
despair,
Decades of friendship, an enduring affair.
The world had changed, but their camaraderie
remained the same,
In the fortitude of their friendship, they found
life's truest aim

Grace of Gratitude - Grandma's Memory Box

In her attic, Grandma's box filled with notes,
Daily moments of thanks, life anecdotes.
A smile from a stranger, rain's gentle touch,
Tiny joys she cherished, ever so much.
Through gratitude's lens, her life did shine,
A testament of grace, woven through time.

Harmony of Healing - The Coffee Shop Chronicles

At the coffee shop corner, they sat side by side,
From a union once strong, to a marriage that died.
Yet, sipping their drinks, they now converse free,
Recalling memories, letting past grievances be.
Though heartaches once clouded their vision so clear,
In the harmony of healing, they found a bond still dear.
From love to friendship, their journey did extend,
Although the sun sets over them, endings aren't really the end.

Insights for Inner Child - Shadows to Light

Witness to hurt, in a home that wasn't safe and
sound,
Where love should flourish, but pain was found.
Yet with time and care, he began to see,
Forgiving wasn't forgetting but setting his spirit
free.
He chose healing's path, for his parent and his
heart,
A journey from shadows, a new start.

Journey of Joy - Rediscovering Childhood

In a school visit, where children learned and played,
He watched with a smile, in memories he swayed.
Recollecting his youth, with games and endless joy,
When every moment was cherished, with every toy.
A simple slide ride, or a swing in the air,
Brought back the essence of a time without care.
With children around, he joined in the play,
Rediscovering joy, in a heartfelt way.

Knowledge of Kindness - Office Vibes

In a busy office, where deadlines loomed near,
A leader stressed kindness, making the mission clear.
She set up a "Kindness Board", for all to view,
A space for shoutouts, where appreciation grew.
As days turned to weeks, the board filled with praise,
Transforming the culture, in so many ways.
With every note posted, colleagues began to see,
The power of gratitude, and how uplifting it can be.

Lovingness of Listening - Circles Embrace

In a circle they sat, each voice taking a turn,
Listening intently, there was so much to learn.
One by one, they shared their deepest fears,
With the group's loving ears, wiping away tears.
Through every story, bonds grew stronger,
With the lovingness of listening, they felt
isolated no longer.
Around they went, weaving threads of trust,
In that listening circle, healing was a must.

Multitudes of Mindfulness - Daily Dive

Ten minutes daily, in stillness I stay,
Mindfulness guiding the chaos away.
Breathing in deeply, I let worries release,
In this quiet moment, I find my peace.
Surrounded by calm, the world takes a pause,
In the multitudes of mindfulness, I understand
its cause.
Through this daily ritual, clarity I find,
A tranquil journey, for heart and mind.

Nourishment of Now –
Thriving while balancing

In the office hustle, I find my space,
Enjoying every challenge, at my own pace.
The "now" teaches me to balance and thrive,
Learning new things, feeling truly alive.
Immersed in work, yet always in the present,
Each task is a joy, every moment is pleasant.
The nourishment of now fuels my days dance,
Embracing each moment, in work and in trance.

Opulence of Open-mindedness - His Transformation

In a sheltered world, his beliefs were confined,
Only known norms, in his young, molded mind.
But exposure brought richness, perspectives anew,
Understanding gender, faiths, and varied hues.
From rigid thoughts to an embrace so grand,
The opulence of open-mindedness, he came to understand.

Power of Play - Remembering Their Way

They found solace in laughter and dice,
In the heart of the city, amidst all the vice.
Board games at dusk, football during the day,
Through the power of play, they would always
sway.
With every chuckle, stress began to fray,
In their playful world, we all wished to stay.

Quest for Quietude- In the Park

In the park, surrounded by nature's tone,
She sat on a bench, truly alone.
With birds above and grass below,
She chose mindfulness over her phone.
Embracing the moment, present and known,
She found peace, in being truly on her own

Radiance of Reflection- Sea's Gentle Guide

By the sea's vast expanse, I took a chance,
Listening to waves, in introspection's dance.
Their rhythmic whispers, truths did convey,
Guiding my soul, showing the way.
In this deep reflection, my path became clear,
Living authentically, with purpose so dear.

Symphony of Service - The Volunteer's Tune

I observed a volunteer, with children she'd kneel,
Guiding those with special needs, her compassion real.
Helping young ones rise, from setbacks they faced,
Her dedication, a melody, in challenges embraced.
In her harmonious service, my heart found a guide,
Witnessing love in action, with pride amplified.

Tenderness of Therapy - The Right Fit

For years I wandered, seeking a guiding light,
Through therapists' doors, hoping for insight.
Until one day, in a room so serene,
I found the therapist where my soul felt seen.
In their tenderness, my healing journey began,
Grateful for the search that led to this plan.

Unboxing Understanding - A Fresh Start

As she delved deep into her heart's core,
She understood her parents like never before.
With newfound clarity, past resentments did
fade,
Choosing to let go, a new path she laid.
Embracing tomorrow, with memories anew,
She took steps forward, to herself she stayed
true.

Virtues of Vulnerability - A Personal Unveiling

Embracing vulnerability, I took a bold stance,
Shedding jealousy, giving growth a chance.
Toxic masculinity, I chose to defy,
With an open heart, old burdens did fly.
By being true to myself, I started to heal,
In vulnerability's grace, I found what's real.

Wonders of Wholesomeness - The Heartfelt Friend

In my dear friend's embrace, wholesomeness
shines,
Every hug, a reminder, where true love aligns.
Simple gestures, warm laughter, nights so long,
With her genuine spirit, I felt I belonged.
Through each heartfelt gesture and memory,
we've spun,
She embodies the essence of wholesomeness,
second to none.

X-Raying Existence - The Balancing Act

While diving deep, one might stagnate and
freeze,
Lost in reflection, like leaves in a breeze.
Yet, a leader finds balance, reflecting while in
stride,
Merging introspection with action, side by side.
Pondering existence, yet with goals firmly in
traction,
They master the dance of thought and swift
action.

Yielding to Yearning - Embers of Love Renewed

Post-breakup, a heart learns to yield,
Embracing solitude, wounds slowly healed.
Yet in time, yearnings awake and begin,
To hope for love's dance, once again.

Zestful Zeal - Inspiring Journeys Unveiled

In every endeavor, their zeal shines so clear,
Juggling passions, conquering every fear.
With undying zest, through challenges they
weave,
Embracing life's dance, in what they believe.
Their spirit, unyielding, forever remains,
A beacon of hope, through life's joys and pains.